The BEING Zone

"Sharing her own story of transformation and over 100 journaling exercises to empower readers, Marla Williams' heartfelt The BEING Zone is a sensitive guidebook that will take you on a journey of personal healing and discovery."

~Theresa Nicassio PhD, Psychologist, Wellness Educator, Radio Host, and Award-Winning Author of *YUM: Plant-Based Recipes for a Gluten-Free Diet*

"Marla's encouragement to journal has been key to transforming my life. Physically writing down old hurts was painful but helped me identify unresolved issues to release and heal. I am feeling happier than I have in years."

~Trudie German, Online Personal Trainer, Health and Fitness Speaker, Corporate Wellness Specialist, Owner of Body Envy

"Let your words flow from your beating heart directly to your hands. The healing that happens when you leave your head and simply write from your heart is lifechanging."

~Loretta Friesen, Founder, Alynemint Coaching and Consulting

"Journaling is the game-changer. When I can write out all my fears, feelings and beliefs, everything becomes much clearer for me. It is an ideal place to think, feel, discover, expand, remember and dream."

~Rachel Strong, *BEING Zone* Client

THE BEING JOURNAL

Your Companion Book to The BEING Zone™

A Tool for Journaling Your Way Through
Rediscovery, Reconnection, and Healing

Marla Williams and Amanda Stovall

Support@TheBEINGZone.com
www.TheBEINGZone.com
The BEING Zone™

Ordering Information:
Quantity sales. Special discounts are available on quantity purchases by non-profits. For details, contact the publisher at the email address above.
Printed in the United States of America

Co-Authored by Marla Williams and Amanda Stovall
The BEING Journal: A Companion Book to The BEING Zone: A Tool for Journaling Your Way through Rediscovery, Reconnection, and Healing.

Cover Design by John Browning
Illustrations by Amanda Stovall
Interior Design by Colleen Sheehan

The names and identifying details in the client stories that follow have been changed to protect the privacy of individuals. Except for a few clients who wanted their story told.

The information contained in this book does not constitute medical advice. It is meant as a source of valuable information for the reader but is not a substitute for direct expert assistance. Please consult with your physician or medical professional to determine what may be best for your individual needs.

Journal ISBN 978-1-7349253-2-6

First Edition

We dedicate this book to anyone who is struggling in life and the practitioners who dedicate their lives to helping them. We know it takes an open mind and heart to have the courage to take this journey of transformation. We are grateful for our friends, family, and clients for their ongoing encouragement and support.

TABLE OF

Contents

Introduction

"Silence is a source of great strength."
—Lao Tzu

*T*HIS *BEING JOURNAL* is the companion notebook to *The BEING Zone™* book which provides a transformational system for self-discovery, reconnection, and healing. This *BEING Journal* has been developed because journaling is an essential part of the healing process. Your commitment to journaling throughout this program is your gateway to transformation.

Journaling is a proven method of self-care, as studies have shown journaling is a way to bring calm to chaos by taking inner turmoil and transferring it to paper. You'll find releasing memories from your mind and out your fingertips will have unmatched therapeutic and cathartic value.

Journaling will allow you to uncover (or unearth) your story and identify life experiences that are affecting you today, as well as help you get clarity on creating the future you desire. Be as honest and real as you can and let out your stories, so they can reach the light of day. You'll start to understand how your life experiences are affecting you today and will be able to make conscious decisions to clear away negative patterns and beliefs that have remained within you.

This *BEING Journal* will mirror chapter by chapter *The BEING Zone* book. As you read *The BEING Zone* you will be alerted to complete a journal activity. Follow along in your book and be as thorough and long winded as you want—this is truly the time to let things out. Sometimes stories can be painful and may bring out some unpleasantness—rest assured if you are reading the book you will have exercises to help you through the difficult experiences along the way. There are open journaling pages at the end of the book if you don't have enough room to journal on any of the questions.

Let your *BEING Zone Journey* begin! We applaud you for taking time to take care of yourself.

PART I

Why We Are the Way We Are and What We Can Do About It

Our Disconnected World

"These pains you feel are messengers. Listen to them."
—Rumi

I N C H A P T E R 1 of *The BEING Zone* book, you are
learning about trauma and technology and how the subconscious mind has impacted your happiness and well-being in
the world. Many people are suffering in some regard, whether it
be loneliness, feeling disconnected, frustration, stress—this list
goes on and on. When you exist in these places of unhappiness
you may not be able to fully experience unconditional self-love
and connection with yourself and others. The journal activities in
Chapter 1 will help you become aware of issues you may have in
relation to trauma, technology, and disconnection. You might be

shocked by some of the statistics you read about, or maybe you are already aware of what is going on in our world. This first chapter can be really eye opening either way. There will be some exercises to shed light on how your past is affecting you today. You will begin to learn about who you are and take notice of how you react to certain situations.

Journaling Time

PSYCHOLOGICAL ABUSE OR TRAUMA JOURNALING EXERCISE #1:

What are the things that were said to you as a child that affected your happiness, your confidence, your well-being or belief system?

_____

_____

_____

_____

_____

_____

_____

What things did you hear growing up that made you feel small or incapable or not enough?

_____

_____

_____

_____

_____

_____

_____

Take yourself back to those early years and brainstorm all the innocuous comments that may have caused you to feel inadequate, dismissed, or unimportant. It is important to capture all that you can so we can clear them from your psyche when you learn the tools in Chapter 3.

_____

_____

_____

_____

_____

_____

_____

_____

_____

_____

_____

_____

_____

_____

_____

_____

_____

_____

_____

Journaling Time

The A.C.E. Study Journaling Exercise #2:

Review the A.C.E. Study Chart on page 23-24 of *The BEING Zone* book and identify anything from their list that may have impacted you.

_____

_____

_____

_____

_____

_____

Write out as much as you can about each of the different types of abuse or trauma you may have faced throughout your life.

_____

_____

_____

_____

_____

_____

_____

_____

Make enough notes so that you can gain clarity about how it has impacted you
so you can come back and clear these issues after learning the tools.

_____

_____

_____

_____

_____

_____

_____

_____

_____

_____

_____

_____

_____

_____

_____

_____

_____

_____

_____

_____

Journaling Time

REVIEW DATA ON VIOLENCE AND RAPE JOURNALING EXERCISE #3:

First, review the Hamby, Taggart and Rainn studies and facts on pages 25-27 of *The BEING Zone* book and identify anything from the statistics that may have impacted you.

_____

_____

_____

_____

_____

_____

_____

_____

_____

_____

_____

_____

_____

_____

_____

_____

_____

Then write out as much as you can about each of the different types of violence you may have faced throughout your life. Get clarity about how it has impacted you so can clear the issues when you learn the tools.

_____

_____

_____

_____

_____

_____

_____

_____

_____

_____

_____

_____

_____

_____

_____

_____

_____

_____

_____

_____

_____

Journaling Time

GENERAL OR SPECIFIC EVENTS JOURNALING EXERCISE #4:

First, review the Specific and General Events on page 30 of *The BEING Zone* book and identify any that may have impacted you.

_____

_____

_____

_____

_____

_____

_____

_____

_____

_____

_____

_____

_____

_____

_____

_____

_____

_____

Then write out as much as you can about your memories in each area. Make enough notes so that you can gain clarity about how it has impacted you. If you experienced none of these, keep reading.

_____

_____

_____

_____

_____

_____

_____

_____

_____

_____

_____

_____

_____

_____

_____

_____

_____

_____

Journaling Time

Triggers Journaling Exercise #5:

What types of things trigger you?

_____

_____

_____

_____

_____

_____

_____

Who are people who trigger you?

_____

_____

_____

_____

_____

_____

_____

What are you struggling with in life as a result of how you were treated in childhood?

_____

_____

_____

_____

_____

_____

_____

What memories and struggles have you pushed under the carpet because they feel so painful?

_____

_____

_____

_____

_____

_____

_____

_____

_____

_____

_____

Journaling Time

SYMPTOMS JOURNALING EXERCISE #6:

List the different emotional, psychological or physical symptoms or beliefs from the examples listed on pages 34 and 35 of *The BEING Zone* book that are currently a part of you and your life.

_____

_____

_____

_____

_____

_____

Make a note of which of these you experience a lot and how it impacts you. This will assist you in identifying what to clear when you get to Chapter 3.

_____

_____

_____

_____

_____

_____

Journaling Time

SIMPLE ACTIVITIES FOR CLEARING TRAUMA JOURNALING EXERCISE #7:

Create a list of any of the simple activities for clearing trauma listed on pages 35 and 36 of *The BEING Zone* book that would be useful in your life right now. Feel free to add your own ideas for activities that may be helpful to you.

_____

_____

_____

_____

_____

_____

Make notes on how any of these activities might help and what you are ready to commit to.

_____

_____

_____

_____

_____

_____

_____

Journaling Time

POTENTIAL PTSD ISSUES JOURNALING EXERCISE #8:

Write about events in your life that you can't let go of and are continuing to impact you years later.

_____

_____

_____

_____

_____

_____

_____

_____

_____

_____

_____

_____

_____

_____

_____

_____

Make a note of which of these you experience a lot and describe how. This will assist you on your healing journey, when you use the tools shared in Chapter 3 to help clear these issues.

_____

_____

_____

_____

_____

_____

_____

_____

_____

_____

_____

_____

_____

_____

_____

_____

_____

_____

_____

_____

Journaling Time

TECHNOLOGY ADDICTIONS JOURNALING EXERCISE #9:

Think about the last time you witnessed a family or group of friends sitting with their faces in their phones instead of having conversations. What were they missing out on?

_____

_____

_____

_____

_____

Have you experienced someone who disrupts your conversation by responding to a text message or email when you're mid-sentence? How does that make you feel?

_____

_____

_____

_____

_____

_____

Has there been a time you wanted to have a serious conversation with someone, but they couldn't stay focused because of technical distractions? Describe these events. How did you feel or respond?

_____

_____

_____

_____

_____

_____

_____

_____

How often are you on your phone or technology where it impacts others? Describe the situation. What can you do about that?

_____

_____

_____

_____

_____

_____

_____

How often do you work into your personal or family time? Does your work ever make it difficult to enjoy your life at home? Have you seen this in your family or friends?

_____

_____

_____

_____

_____

_____

_____

_____

_____

What would you like to change about the role technology plays in your relationships?

_____

_____

_____

_____

_____

_____

_____

_____

Journaling Time

TECHNOLOGY USE JOURNALING EXERCISE #10:

How many total hours do you spend in an average day using technology?

_____

_____

_____

_____

How much time do you spend online doing each of the following: Gaming? Research-
ing for fun or educational purposes? Working? Browsing social media? Describe
your situation.

_____

_____

_____

How many hours a week do you spend watching TV or streaming videos on average?
Describe your tendencies.

_____

_____

_____

_____

How many hours a week do you spend socializing with friends or family? Describe those times you love. What are you doing? Who are you with?

_____

_____

_____

_____

_____

_____

_____

_____

If you are in a relationship, how many hours a week do you spend in quality time with your significant other, where you are in person and having an actual conversation?

_____

_____

_____

_____

_____

_____

_____

_____

How many hours do you spend doing extracurricular activities with others, such as exercise, sports, volunteering, group activities, spiritual worship, or at specific events?

_____

_____

_____

_____

_____

_____

_____

Are all your activities balanced in your life? If not, what changes can you make? What can you commit to?

_____

_____

_____

_____

_____

_____

_____

_____

Ingrained Beliefs And Blocks

"Every adversity, every failure, every heartache carries
with it the seed of an equal or greater benefit."
—Napoleon Hill

I N CHAPTER 2, you discover that you were born perfect
and, in the beginning, you followed your heart's desires.
Over time that changes. For some of you it may have been a long,
slow process that didn't have too much of an impact on you. For
others, it may have happened rather quickly as your home life may
have been very challenging. Many life experiences have the ability
to take you away from who you really are at the core. Your struggles
or negative life experiences had the ability to create self-defeat-
ing beliefs or emotional blocks and barriers, essentially creating

filters to alter your perception of the way life is. As you read on, you will find you are more than the sum total of your outward achievements and can begin to heal when you remove the emotional blocks holding you back. The journaling in this chapter will assist you in exploring your life's journey so far, by going back to your childhood to discover what caused you pain or made you feel bad. Identifying negative programming, beliefs, trauma and memories is the first step in uncovering core issues that are holding you in place. Once you get through this chapter you will be well on your way to being able to start creating a life you desire by feeling less triggered and frustrated, and more peaceful and calm inside.

Journaling Time

BIRTH TO AGE 5 JOURNALING EXERCISE #11:

What do you remember from those years? What stories have you heard from family members or friends?

_____

_____

_____

_____

_____

_____

_____

_____

_____

_____

_____

_____

_____

_____

_____

_____

_____

_____

Describe any memories of being yelled at, scolded, spanked, or struck.

_____

_____

_____

_____

_____

_____

_____

_____

_____

Explain any memories of being reprimanded for doing things you loved.

_____

_____

_____

_____

_____

_____

_____

_____

_____

_____

_____

_____

Write about things you were told such as: You are not enough or not smart enough, etc.

_____

_____

_____

_____

_____

_____

_____

_____

Write down any memories about being locked in your room or sent to bed without dinner and how that felt to you.

_____

_____

_____

_____

_____

_____

_____

_____

Detail out any memories you have around having tantrums or wetting your bed.

_____

_____

_____

_____

_____

_____

_____

_____

Identify and describe any negative beliefs or blocks that may have come from one of the above incidents.

_____

_____

_____

_____

_____

_____

_____

Journaling Time

GRADE SCHOOL JOURNALING EXERCISE #12:

What are your hardest or most painful memories from those years?

_____

_____

_____

_____

_____

_____

_____

Were there teachers or others in positions of authority who embarrassed or belittled you? Describe how you were—or still are—influenced by those situations.

_____

_____

_____

_____

_____

_____

Were there kids who bullied you? If so, how did that make you feel?

_____

_____

_____

_____

_____

_____

Describe situations where teachers, peers, or family members were mean or rude to you and how it felt.

_____

_____

_____

_____

_____

_____

Did you ever get left out and feel hurt deep inside? Describe the memory.

_____

_____

_____

_____

_____

_____

Did you feel supported by your family? Explain why or why not.

_____

_____

_____

_____

_____

Can you identify any negative beliefs or blocks you have today that may have come from one or more of these experiences?

_____

_____

_____

_____

_____

What activities did you enjoy doing at this age? Where did you get lost in the moment? Do you still enjoy any of these today?

_____

_____

_____

_____

_____

Journaling Time

MIDDLE SCHOOL YEARS JOURNALING EXERCISE #13:

What were your greatest insecurities at the time?

_____

_____

_____

_____

_____

What are your greatest regrets now, looking back?

_____

_____

_____

_____

_____

How important was it to you to be cool or accepted by the popular kids?

_____

_____

_____

_____

Were there things you did, or risks you took, that looking back you wish you hadn't done? If so, explain.

_____

_____

_____

_____

_____

Were you telling your parents—or maybe yourself—lies about what you were doing or how you felt?

_____

_____

_____

_____

_____

Write about any specific times when you didn't stand up for yourself or say no.

_____

_____

_____

_____

_____

Can you identify and explain any beliefs or blocks that came from a child-hood experience?

_____

_____

_____

_____

_____

_____

What activities did you enjoy doing at this age? Where did you get lost in the moment? Do you still enjoy any of these today?

_____

_____

_____

_____

_____

_____

_____

_____

_____

_____

_____

_____

_____

Journaling Time

HIGH SCHOOL YEARS JOURNALING EXERCISE #14:

What are your worst memories or regrets? List them and write what you remember.

_____

_____

_____

_____

_____

_____

_____

Do you remember anything said or done to you that made you hurt or feel left out? Take time to write about those times.

_____

_____

_____

_____

_____

_____

_____

Were there times you were in situations you knew were wrong, but you didn't have the confidence, strength, or power to walk away? Explain.

_____

_____

_____

_____

_____

_____

_____

_____

Can you identify any negative beliefs or blocks you have today that may have come from one or more of these experiences? What are they?

_____

_____

_____

_____

_____

_____

_____

_____

_____

Did you feel confident, loved, supported, and encouraged to follow your heart? If not, explain.

_____

_____

_____

_____

_____

_____

_____

_____

_____

Do you still feel like you are living your dream? If no, why not?

_____

_____

_____

_____

_____

_____

_____

_____

_____

_____

What activities did you enjoy doing at this age? Where did you get lost in the moment? Do you still enjoy any of these today?

_____

_____

_____

_____

_____

_____

_____

_____

_____

_____

_____

_____

_____

_____

_____

_____

_____

_____

_____

_____

_____

Journaling Time

College Years to Now Journaling Exercise #15:

Were the life decisions you've made based on ensuring your safety or security or did they consider what makes you happy and fills you up? Describe.

_____

_____

_____

_____

_____

_____

_____

_____

_____

_____

_____

_____

_____

_____

Looking back, what were your worst memories or pains during your adult years? Why are these memories so hurtful?

_____

_____

_____

_____

_____

_____

_____

Did you ever get fired from a job or laid off? How did that make you feel?

_____

_____

_____

_____

_____

_____

_____

_____

Were you ever treated disrespectfully or incorrectly in a work environment? How did it feel?

_____

_____

_____

_____

_____

Were you ever treated as if you weren't good enough or not smart enough? Or passed over for a promotion when you were the best candidate? Describe how that felt.

_____

_____

_____

_____

_____

Can you identify and describe any negative beliefs or blocks you have today that may have come from one or more of these experiences?

_____

_____

_____

_____

_____

What other memories do you have that you would like to clear?

_____

_____

_____

_____

_____

What activities did you enjoy doing at this age? Where did you get lost in the moment? Do you still enjoy any of these today?

_____

_____

_____

_____

_____

_____

_____

_____

_____

_____

_____

_____

_____

_____

_____

Journaling Time

CURRENT LIFE OBSERVATIONS JOURNALING EXERCISE #16:

Do you love your life? Are you fulfilled? Describe what, why, and how.

_____

_____

_____

_____

_____

_____

_____

If you were to stop and tune into what you really wanted your life to be like, what would you see or hear?

_____

_____

_____

_____

_____

_____

_____

What would you like to do differently now that you are increasing your awareness?

_____

_____

_____

_____

_____

_____

_____

_____

What beliefs in your life are stopping you from stepping into your power?

_____

_____

_____

_____

_____

_____

_____

_____

_____

_____

_____

_____

_____

Journaling Time

LIFE HAPPINESS JOURNALING EXERCISE #17:

Is money or happiness more important to you? Why?

_____

_____

_____

_____

_____

_____

_____

_____

How many people do you know who live in the survival state and just get by? Are you one of those? Describe how your life feels if you are operating in this way.

_____

_____

_____

_____

_____

_____

How many people do you know who don't love their life or their job? How about you? Describe your situation.

_____

_____

_____

_____

_____

_____

_____

What do you love about your life and job? What do you dislike?

_____

_____

_____

_____

_____

_____

_____

_____

_____

_____

_____

_____

Journaling Time

HEALTH BELIEFS JOURNALING EXERCISE #18:

If your parents were (or are) overweight, do you believe that will be your reality?
Describe how that has impacted you and your life.

_____

_____

_____

_____

_____

_____

If any of your family members has or had heart disease or cancer, do you expect
that you will, also? Describe your current fears and how you can change those
beliefs.

_____

_____

_____

_____

_____

_____

_____

What other illnesses or diseases do you feel you are predisposed to as a result of family beliefs? Now do some online research asking what diseases are genetic. The list is short. You will be able to eliminate many fears.

_____

_____

_____

_____

_____

_____

_____

_____

It is essential to clear these old beliefs as part of your healing process. Make a list of what you need to clear.

_____

_____

_____

_____

_____

_____

_____

_____

_____

5 WHYS ON EACH NEGATIVE BELIEF OR BLOCK JOURNALING EXERCISE #19:

Ask yourself and document the "5 Whys" on each negative belief or block you identified or on why you feel like you do in your life.

_____

_____

_____

_____

_____

_____

_____

_____

_____

_____

_____

_____

_____

_____

_____

_____

_____

_____

_____

See if you can identify the root cause of your unhappiness through the "5 Whys" process. Then make notes on what you can change to improve how you feel. When you understand it, you'll be ready to *SHIFT* or clear it from your life.

_____

_____

_____

_____

_____

_____

_____

_____

_____

_____

_____

_____

_____

_____

_____

_____

_____

_____

_____

_____

Journaling Time

Summary of Key Learnings Journaling Exercise #20:

Document where you feel the most pain or have negative beliefs or blocks, as those are the ones you should target with the healing tools offered in Chapter 3.

_____

_____

_____

_____

_____

_____

_____

_____

_____

_____

_____

_____

_____

_____

_____

_____

CHAPTER 3

Tools For Clearing Blocks And Beliefs

"Courage is knowing what not to fear."
—Plato

CHAPTER 3 PROVIDES you the tools needed to clear old belief systems, trauma, and blocks in your life. Many options of tools and techniques are given because every individual is unique, and you'll want to experiment to find the ones that work most effectively for your for different types of issues. Try the different exercises and then reflect on how each felt and what worked best. By the end of the chapter you will have identified your most useful tools.

Make a list of the top tools and techniques and for what type of issue they work on. You'll have your own personalized tool kit that you understand, relate to, and can begin to use on a regular basis. You can always refer back to Chapter 3 to see how the different tools may be useful as new situations inevitably come up in your life.

THREE-PART BREATHING JOURNALING EXERCISE #21:

Listen to a recording in Chapter 3 at www.TheBEINGZone.com/tools. Write about how well the Three-Part Breathing exercise worked for you.

_____

_____

_____

_____

_____

_____

Did you feel more centered and calmer? If so, explain how you felt.

_____

_____

_____

_____

_____

_____

_____

_____

If not, how did you feel?

_____

_____

_____

_____

_____

_____

_____

_____

Is this an exercise you will most likely use moving forward?

_____

_____

_____

_____

_____

_____

_____

_____

_____

_____

_____

_____

_____

Journaling Time

MINDFUL BREATHING JOURNALING EXERCISE #22:

Listen to the Mindful Breathing recording at www.TheBEINGZone.com/tools in Chapter 3. Make notes on how well the Mindful Breathing exercise worked for you.

_____

_____

_____

_____

_____

How did it make you feel? Do you feel more peaceful or tranquil?

_____

_____

_____

_____

_____

Do you feel this is an exercise you will most likely use moving forward?

_____

_____

Journaling Time

BREATHE INTO IT AND SURRENDER JOURNALING EXERCISE #23:

Listen to the recording at www.TheBEINGZone.com/tools. Write about how well the Breathe Into It and Surrender exercise worked for you.

_____

_____

_____

_____

_____

_____

_____

Describe how it felt in your body.

_____

_____

_____

_____

_____

_____

Did you feel a release of pain or anger? Describe the feeling of that release.

_____

_____

_____

_____

_____

_____

_____

_____

Is this an exercise you will most likely use moving forward? Explain how.

_____

_____

_____

_____

_____

_____

_____

_____

_____

_____

Journaling Time

TAPPING OR EFT JOURNALING EXERCISE #24:

Listen to the tapping recording at www.TheBEINGZone.com/tools. Write about how well the tapping exercise worked for you.

_____

_____

_____

_____

_____

_____

Did you feel lighter overall from the experience? Describe how that felt.

_____

_____

_____

_____

_____

_____

Did you feel a release? If so, how would you describe it?

_____

_____

_____

_____

_____

_____

_____

_____

_____

Will you use this tool? Make notes on the types of situations where this tool may be most useful to you.

_____

_____

_____

_____

_____

_____

_____

_____

_____

Journaling Time

HEALING CODE JOURNALING EXERCISE #25:

Listen to the Healing Codes recording at www.TheBEINGZone.com/tools.
Write about how well the Healing Codes exercise worked for you.

_____

_____

_____

_____

_____

_____

_____

Did you feel different afterwards? Describe how.

_____

_____

_____

_____

_____

_____

_____

_____

Did you feel less frustrated or defeated? Describe what you were able to release.

_____

_____

_____

_____

_____

_____

_____

_____

Is this an exercise you will most likely use moving forward? Explain how.

_____

_____

_____

_____

_____

_____

_____

_____

_____

_____

Journaling Time

SUBCONSCIOUS SUGGESTION PROCESS JOURNALING EXERCISE #26:

Review pages 92-93 for this process in *The BEING Zone* book. Write about how well the Subconscious Suggestion Process exercise worked for you.

_____

_____

_____

_____

_____

_____

_____

_____

_____

_____

_____

_____

_____

_____

_____

_____

_____

_____

Did you sleep well? Did you have any dreams? Did you wake up feeling different? Write about your experience.

_____

_____

_____

_____

_____

_____

_____

_____

Do you think this is a useful tool moving forward?

_____

_____

_____

_____

_____

_____

_____

_____

_____

_____

_____

Journaling Time

POND EXERCISE TO RECONNECT WITH INNER CHILD
AND RELEASE JOURNALING EXERCISE #27:

Make notes on how well the Pond Exercise to Reconnect with Inner Child and Release exercise worked for you. Go to www.TheBEINGZone.com/tools to listen.

_____

_____

_____

_____

_____

_____

_____

_____

_____

_____

_____

_____

_____

_____

Do you feel you were able to let go of old issues? Write about what you feel different about.

_____

_____

_____

_____

_____

_____

_____

_____

Did you feel lighter afterwards? Describe what that feels like in your body.

_____

_____

_____

_____

_____

_____

_____

_____

_____

_____

_____

Do you feel you have more people to forgive or were you able to address most issues in your life? Make notes on who else you need to forgive and release in your life.

_____

_____

_____

_____

_____

_____

_____

_____

_____

_____

_____

Is this an exercise you will most likely use again?

_____

_____

_____

_____

_____

_____

Journaling Time

THE MIND-BODY CONNECTION JOURNALING EXERCISE #28:

Do you have any chronic aches or pains in your body? Describe what those are. Revisit pages 97-99 in *The BEING Zone* book for a reminder of this process.

_____

_____

_____

_____

_____

_____

_____

Do you have any untold stories or traumatic memories that you can share that will help release those chronic aches or pains?

_____

_____

_____

_____

_____

_____

_____

Follow the example above and write about how well the Mind-Body Connection exercise worked for you.

_____

_____

_____

_____

_____

_____

_____

_____

Were you able to let go of any old pains or aches? Describe those.

_____

_____

_____

_____

_____

_____

_____

_____

_____

Did you feel better or lighter afterwards? Describe the difference you felt.

_____

_____

_____

_____

_____

_____

_____

_____

_____

Do you feel that this will a valuable tool in your toolbox?

_____

_____

_____

_____

_____

_____

_____

_____

_____

Journaling Time

THE *SHIFT* TOOL JOURNALING EXERCISE #29:

Please take the time to experience this tool as it is one of the most powerful tools in this book. It is one we highly recommend you have in your toolbox.

Write about your experience after utilizing the *SHIFT* Tool recording in Chapter 3 at www.TheBEINGZone.com/tools. Some people will feel a major *SHIFT* and some not so much. Write about how you felt. The more you practice and use this tool, the more powerful it will become.

_____

_____

_____

_____

_____

_____

_____

_____

_____

_____

_____

_____

Did you feel better or lighter afterwards? Describe the differences you feel.

_____

_____

_____

_____

_____

_____

_____

_____

_____

_____

_____

_____

_____

_____

_____

_____

_____

_____

_____

_____

_____

_____

_____

_____

_____

Journaling Time

THE PSYCH-K JOURNALING EXERCISE #30:

Were you able to find a PSYCH-K practitioner to help you with this? If so, write about how well the PSYCH-K tool worked for you. Review the method on page 103 of *The BEING Zone* book or go to www.psych-k.com/ to learn more.

_____

_____

_____

If you experienced the tool, did you feel a change in how you felt?

_____

_____

_____

_____

Is this an exercise you will most likely use moving forward?

_____

_____

_____

If you didn't experience this process, move onto the next journaling exercise.

Journaling Time

THE THETAHEALING JOURNALING EXERCISE #31:

Were you able to find a ThetaHealing practitioner to help you with this? If so, make notes on how well the ThetaHealing process worked for you. Learn more on page 105 of *The BEING Zone* book or go to www.Thetahealing.com.

_____

_____

_____

_____

_____

If you experienced the process, did you feel a change in how you felt and is this an exercise you will most likely use moving forward?

_____

_____

_____

_____

_____

If you didn't experience this process, move onto the next journaling exercise.

PART II

Steps to Transformation

CHAPTER 4

A Heart-Based Life

"The best and most beautiful things in the world cannot be
seen or even touched—they must be felt with the heart."
—Helen Keller

IN CHAPTER 4, you learn how to how to turn off "that
voice," the one you hear over and over, full of negative
thoughts and emotions that can dominate your daily life. You learn
how to tune into your body, and listen to and follow your intuition. The journal activities in Chapter 4 will help you become
aware of your thoughts, passed down belief systems, and how to
become mindful of the impact your ego has on you. You'll have an
easier time navigating your life once you are cognizant of this information and integrate the heart-based activities into your daily life.

Journaling Time

THOUGHTS BECOME THINGS JOURNALING EXERCISE #32:

What thoughts do you have day after day?

_____

_____

_____

_____

_____

_____

_____

Note which are positive and which are harmful or draining.

_____

_____

_____

_____

_____

_____

_____

How do your harmful or negative thoughts impact your life?

_____

_____

_____

_____

_____

_____

_____

What do you want your reality to be without thinking about current limitations?

_____

_____

_____

_____

_____

_____

_____

What tools can you use to change your thoughts?

_____

_____

_____

_____

Journaling Time

CHANGE SUBCONSCIOUS THOUGHTS TO CONSCIOUS THOUGHTS JOURNALING EXERCISE #33:

Write about what you seem to complain about and things you feel are unjust or unfair. Who do you blame?

_____

_____

_____

_____

_____

_____

_____

_____

_____

_____

_____

_____

_____

_____

_____

_____

_____

_____

What negative thoughts do you consistently have? List these in the left column.

In the right column, replace the negative thoughts with thankfulness for a new Conscious thought of what you do want to focus on instead.

EXAMPLES OF SUBCONSCIOUS THOUGHTS	EXAMPLES OF CONSCIOUS THOUGHTS TO FOCUS ON
My son leaves a mess in the kitchen every day.	I am thankful my son has begun to leave a clean kitchen each day.

Will you use this tool again? When might it be helpful to you?

_____

_____

_____

_____

_____

_____

_____

_____

_____

_____

_____

_____

_____

_____

_____

_____

_____

_____

_____

_____

Journaling Time

BELIEF SYSTEMS JOURNALING EXERCISE #34:

What beliefs do you feel were passed down to you? They may be religious beliefs or beliefs about how to treat people or a feeling that your family always struggles.

_____

_____

_____

_____

_____

_____

_____

What stories did you hear or do you tell yourself that built up these beliefs?

_____

_____

_____

_____

_____

_____

_____

_____

Do your beliefs impact how you show up in life? Do you flow more through life or push your way through life because of your beliefs?

_____

_____

_____

_____

_____

_____

What beliefs do you want to change?

_____

_____

_____

_____

_____

Was this a useful exercise for you?

_____

_____

_____

_____

_____

_____

Journaling Time

EGO EVALUATION JOURNALING EXERCISE #35:

Highlight all the items from the Ego list that you do even a little bit of the time. It is OK to mark yes on all of them as this is what will help you identify what to begin to recognize in your habits and let go of them.

EGO EVALUATION

Emotions

Worry	Bored	Fear
Anxiety	Dissatisfied	Defensive
Stress	Resentment	Unhappy
Anger	Annoyed	Defeated

Patterns

Guilt	Unexpressed Feelings	Need to Play the Game
Shame	No Power, No Control	Need to Be Liked
Projecting	Manipulate Situations	Critical
Blaming	Live in Past or Future	Judgmental
Complaining	Experience Same Problems Over and Over	Label Others

| Afraid of Rejection | Depressed | Consistent Pain in Body |
| Stifle Emotions | Need to Be in Control | Sabotage Yourself |

Beliefs

Powerless	Seek Approval	Bad Person
Should/Would/ Could Have	Seek Acceptance	Something Wrong with You
Pleaser	Unworthy	Not Enough
Self-Doubt	Not Valued	Never Good Enough

Make notes on which ones you do the most as those are the ones you want to focus on first.

_____

_____

_____

_____

_____

_____

_____

_____

_____

_____

_____

_____

Create a list of your tendencies so you stay aware of when they show up so you can address them when you feel them and begin to eliminate them from your life.

_____

_____

_____

_____

_____

_____

_____

_____

_____

_____

_____

_____

_____

_____

_____

_____

_____

_____

_____

_____

Journaling Time

THROW IT AWAY JOURNALING EXERCISE #36:

There is a recording of the Throw It Away tool at www.TheBEINGZone.com/ tools. Describe how you feel after using this tool: relief, feel lighter, change in energy? Provide as much detail as you can.

_____

_____

_____

_____

_____

What areas do you want to make a commitment to continue to work on?

_____

_____

_____

_____

Will you continue to use this tool?

_____

_____

Journaling Time

CATCH YOURSELF AND WRITE IT DOWN JOURNALING EXERCISE #37:

Were you able to catch yourself thinking negative thoughts? If so, how did you do that?

_____

_____

_____

_____

_____

_____

What was that process like for you?

_____

_____

_____

_____

Do you feel it is something you can build into your life? If so, make notes on how.

_____

_____

_____

Describe how you might use this tool to create positive thought patterns.

_____

_____

_____

_____

_____

What are the other tools in this book that you feel might be effective in helping
you *SHIFT* this negative thought pattern? List them here.

_____

_____

_____

_____

_____

_____

_____

_____

_____

_____

_____

_____

_____

_____

Journaling Time

TURN IT OFF JOURNALING EXERCISE #38:

Could you Turn It Off just like that? Describe what happened.

_____

_____

_____

_____

_____

Describe how you feel after using this tool.

_____

_____

_____

_____

_____

How easy do you think it will be to use this tool in the future?

_____

_____

_____

_____

Journaling Time

ANGEL VERSUS DEVIL JOURNALING EXERCISE #39:

Review the technique on page 128 of *The BEING Zone* book. Make notes on how the Angel Versus Devil technique worked for you.

_____

_____

_____

_____

_____

Describe how effective this tool was for you.

_____

_____

_____

_____

Could you visualize the angel and the devil?

_____

_____

_____

_____

Did you feel your heart warm thinking of the angel? Could you feel the heaviness of the devil?

_____

_____

_____

_____

_____

_____

_____

_____

How do you think you might use this tool in the future?

_____

_____

_____

_____

_____

_____

_____

_____

_____

_____

_____

Journaling Time

IDENTIFYING TRIGGERS AND BELIEFS JOURNALING EXERCISE #40:

Identify and write down your top one to three emotional triggers that you learned about on pages 129-130 of *The BEING Zone* book.

_____

_____

_____

_____

_____

_____

_____

What causes you to be most upset and thrown off balance in relation to those triggers?

_____

_____

_____

_____

_____

Can you remember the first time in your life when you were triggered and felt this way emotionally? This is the memory you want to clear because it will clear all the related incidents that followed it.

_____

_____

_____

_____

_____

_____

_____

What are your underlying belief systems that cause you conflict in your life?

_____

_____

_____

_____

What is your earliest memory of conflict from this belief system? This is what you want to clear as it affects all related future incidents.

_____

_____

_____

_____

_____

_____

Go back and use the *SHIFT* tool, the EFT tool, or another tool of your choosing on the earliest memory related to each trigger point and belief system. Write about your results.

_____

_____

_____

_____

_____

_____

_____

_____

_____

_____

_____

Write about how you might incorporate this tool into your life in the future.

_____

_____

_____

_____

_____

Journaling Time

REPROGRAM NEGATIVES BELIEFS JOURNALING EXERCISE #41:

Review page 131 of *The BEING Zone* book and describe what you were able to reprogram and how it impacted your life.

_____

_____

_____

_____

_____

_____

_____

_____

_____

_____

Describe how you plan to use this tool in the future.

_____

_____

_____

Journaling Time

OPEN-HEART MEDITATION JOURNALING EXERCISE #42:

Go to www.TheBEINGZone.com/tools and Chapter 4 to listen to the Open-Heart Meditation recording. How do you feel after doing this meditation? An expansion in energy, good feelings, happier? What else?

_____

_____

_____

_____

_____

_____

_____

_____

_____

How will you use this tool in the future?

_____

_____

_____

_____

_____

Journaling Time

SWAY TEST JOURNALING EXERCISE #43:

Review the process on page 138 of *The BEING Zone* book. Could you feel a slight movement forward or back? Or did you experience no movement at all? If this was the case, you might try again with a more obvious question, like "my name is..." Or was your experience more extreme, which made things clear for you? If so, this may be the tool for you. Describe what that looked like and felt like to you.

_____

_____

_____

_____

_____

_____

_____

How do you see yourself using this tool in the future?

_____

_____

_____

_____

Journaling Time

FINGER MUSCLE TEST #1 JOURNALING EXERCISE #44:

Review this method on page 139-140 of *The BEING Zone* book. Did your fingers hold on truth and release on false? If so, a lot or a little? Was it clear you were getting answers and not forcing your fingers to respond one way or the other? Write about the questions you asked and the results you got.

_____

_____

_____

_____

_____

_____

_____

_____

What kind of situation do you see yourself using this tool in?

_____

_____

_____

Journaling Time

FINGER MUSCLE TEST #2 JOURNALING EXERCISE #45:

Review this method on page 141 of *The BEING Zone* book. Was it easier for you to use and be confident in your results with this different type of muscle testing? Write about the questions you asked and the results you got.

_____

_____

_____

_____

_____

_____

Did your fingers hold on truth and release on false? If yes, did you feel it happened naturally and you weren't forcing the results in any way at all?

_____

_____

_____

_____

_____

_____

Describe the difference you felt between your true and false questions. Did you feel confident in the results?

_____

_____

_____

_____

_____

_____

_____

Will you use this tool again? In what type of situations do you feel it will work best for you?

_____

_____

_____

_____

_____

_____

_____

_____

_____

_____

Journaling Time

WARM HEART JOURNALING EXERCISE #46:

Go to www.TheBEINGZone.com/tools for the Warm Heart recording. Did you feel your heart warm on truth and cool when not true? If not, what did you feel? If you could clearly feel the warmth and felt you got clarity, this may be the tool for you. Describe the questions you asked and results you received.

_____

_____

_____

_____

_____

_____

_____

_____

_____

_____

_____

_____

_____

What was the difference you felt between true and false? Like warming and cooling, or expanding and contracting, or what else?

_____

_____

_____

_____

_____

_____

_____

_____

_____

Describe the situations where it might be useful for you to use this tool again.

_____

_____

_____

_____

_____

_____

_____

_____

_____

CHAPTER 5

Moving To The BEING Zone

"There are moments when all anxiety and stated toil are becalmed in the infinite leisure and repose of nature."
— Henry David Thoreau

In Chapter 5, you learn to clearly understand that your ingrained belief system is a primary reason why you tend to be on the go all the time and operate in what is called the *DOING Zone*. You learn that most of the time in our society we live in a survival state, rarely taking the time to be present with ourselves. You also learn your ingrained beliefs can be updated and you can move into *The BEING Zone*, which is a more natural state for you. These journal exercises will give you the gift of exploring these issues and give you the chance to reflect and make changes to better yourself and your life.

Journaling Time

DO YOU EXIST IN THE *DOING* ZONE JOURNALING EXERCISE #47:

How much time daily do you spend going or *DOING*? This would include things like working, shopping, cleaning, getting projects or chores done, volunteering, driving, etc. List anything you are doing where your mind, body, and spirit are not at rest. Make notes on where your time is spent and how much time on each activity.

_____

_____

_____

_____

_____

_____

_____

_____

_____

_____

_____

_____

_____

Look at total hours in each area so you have a good understanding of what you might want to work on. Highlight the areas where you could make the most progress.

_____

_____

_____

_____

How much of the time do you find your thoughts or words are putting you into worry, stress, or the *DOING Zone?* What type of things are you thinking or saying?

_____

_____

_____

_____

_____

_____

_____

_____

_____

_____

_____

Journaling Time

HEALTH QUESTIONNAIRE JOURNALING EXERCISE #48:

Is your health compromised? What are your symptoms? Write about how much health issues impact your life.

_____

_____

_____

_____

_____

_____

_____

_____

_____

_____

_____

_____

_____

_____

_____

_____

_____

Do you have high blood pressure? High cholesterol? Heart issues? Write about how much health issues impact your life.

_____

_____

_____

_____

_____

_____

_____

_____

Do you lose sleep? Do you have trouble concentrating? How does this affect your life?

_____

_____

_____

_____

_____

Is your memory failing? Do you walk in a room and can't remember why you went there? How often does this happen, and are others noticing? How does this feel to you?

Do you have tension in your neck and shoulders? Do you frequently have headaches? How often does this happen, and what are you doing to decrease these things?

_____

_____

_____

_____

_____

Describe any digestion, stomach issues, or anxiety issues or panic attacks you might experience.

_____

_____

_____

_____

_____

Do you have inflammation in your body? Do you have low-grade fevers? Do you have any autoimmune diseases? Describe what you feel and how it impacts you.

_____

_____

_____

_____

_____

Do you get colds easily or have consistent problems with congestion in your head, throat, or lungs? How does it impact your daily living?

_____

_____

_____

_____

_____

Do you have any aches, pains, or issues in your back, legs, or arms? How do these impact your life?

_____

_____

_____

_____

_____

Do you get depressed or withdrawn? Describe what happens.

_____

_____

_____

_____

_____

_____

_____

Journaling Time

IMPROVING YOUR HEALTH JOURNALING EXERCISE #49:

Identify the top one or two health issues you want to address and heal from the Health Questionnaire on pages 155 and 156 of *The BEING Zone* book. For each issue, ask yourself what is the underlying root cause of the symptoms?

_____

_____

_____

_____

_____

Search online for "what are the metaphysical reasons I have [this ailment]" and describe what you find.

_____

_____

_____

_____

_____

_____

Once you have identified the metaphysical reason for the ailment, journal ideas on what you can do to overcome these.

_____

_____

_____

_____

_____

_____

_____

_____

_____

_____

_____

_____

_____

_____

_____

_____

_____

_____

Journaling Time

ARE YOU ENGAGED OR COMPULSIVE? JOURNALING EXERCISE #50:

Are you being filled up by your work or depleted? Describe your situation and how you feel about it.

_____

_____

_____

_____

_____

Do you feel more engaged or exhausted when you think about your day at work? Write about how that feels.

_____

_____

_____

_____

_____

_____

_____

Do you tend to be driven and compulsive about what you are doing, or are you lazy and doing as little as possible, or do you just flow through the day with ease? Describe your tendencies.

_____

_____

_____

_____

_____

_____

_____

_____

What might you be able to do to change it for the better?

_____

_____

_____

_____

_____

_____

_____

_____

_____

_____

Journaling Time

WHAT ARE YOUR TENDENCIES JOURNALING EXERCISE #51:

Are you a high achiever who always seems to do more than what seems possible in an eight-hour day? If so, why do you think this is true?

_____

_____

_____

_____

_____

_____

_____

Are you always trying to prove yourself, buy love, or exceed expectations? If so, why and when did this start?

_____

_____

_____

_____

_____

_____

_____

Do you mask any signs of illness with over-the-counter medications? If so, how do you feel about doing that? Is there anything you could change?

_____

_____

_____

_____

_____

_____

_____

_____

Do you lose sleep consistently, so you never feel refreshed? Describe your situation.

_____

_____

_____

_____

_____

_____

_____

_____

_____

_____

Do you keep smiling and pushing even when you are miserable? Write about any memories when you tended to smile and push through instead of being true to yourself.

_____

_____

_____

_____

_____

_____

Do you tune out how you feel or what happens when you feel really emotional?

_____

_____

_____

_____

_____

_____

_____

Do you ever feel depressed, empty, disconnected, or numb? If so, describe
when this happens.

_____

_____

_____

_____

_____

_____

_____

_____

_____

_____

_____

_____

_____

_____

_____

_____

_____

_____

_____

Journaling Time

DOING ZONE SURVEY WRAP UP JOURNALING EXERCISE #52:

What is your score on the survey on page 164 and 165 of *The BEING Zone* book? Why is it at that level?

_____

_____

_____

_____

_____

What can you change in your life to create more work-life balance?

_____

_____

_____

_____

Make a commitment to change at least one thing in your life that will lead you towards the life you desire. Write it down and put in a place to remind you.

_____

_____

Journaling Time

LIST YOUR COMMITMENTS JOURNALING EXERCISE #53:

Make a list of all your current commitments, whether it be work, home, friends, family, community, organizations, etc. Then, highlight all the ones you love doing, that fill you with joy when doing them.

_____

_____

_____

_____

_____

_____

_____

_____

_____

_____

_____

_____

_____

_____

_____

_____

_____

Circle all the items that are not fulfilling or valuable to you. Makes notes on why you circled each item.

_____

_____

_____

_____

_____

_____

Make notes about where you can eliminate, set limits, or decrease the things that that don't make you happy.

_____

_____

_____

_____

_____

_____

_____

Make notes about how balanced your life is and how happy you are.

_____

_____

_____

_____

_____

How much time do you exist in *The BEING Zone* or in the state of joy and synchronicities?

_____

_____

_____

_____

_____

_____

_____

_____

Describe what that looks like and feels like. Identify and write about all the amazing things that happen as a result of living in *The BEING Zone*.

_____

_____

_____

_____

_____

_____

_____

_____

_____

_____

Journaling Time

You Own Your Health Journaling Exercise #54:

List a few of the things where you place your energy every day. What are you focused on? How do you spend your time?

_____

_____

_____

_____

_____

_____

Make notes on the areas of your life that are not changing and where you have pain or stress. These are your areas where you need to learn to disconnect.

_____

_____

_____

_____

_____

_____

How often do you get sick, and what steps do you take to fend it off? Describe all the different situations.

_____

_____

_____

_____

_____

_____

_____

_____

What does your diet look like? Is it nourishing you or depleting you? What can you change?

_____

_____

_____

_____

_____

_____

_____

_____

_____

_____

How much time do you spend feeling good and grounded in life? Describe what and when.

_____

_____

_____

_____

_____

_____

_____

_____

What do you want your life to look like? That's what you should meditate on, think about, and build into your daily thoughts and words.

_____

_____

_____

_____

_____

_____

_____

_____

_____

_____

Journaling Time

ARE YOU LISTENING JOURNALING EXERCISE #55:

Think about any tendencies you may have toward overdoing and not listening to your body's needs. Are there things there you can change?

_____

_____

_____

_____

_____

_____

Write about a time when you pushed yourself beyond what you should have committed to. How did you feel? What were the results?

_____

_____

_____

_____

_____

_____

_____

Think about times when you quit listening to your body and forced yourself to do things you didn't want to do or have time to do. What could you do differently next time?

_____

_____

_____

_____

_____

_____

_____

Journal about things you can do to reboot your mind, body, and soul. You can change your thoughts and words to revamp how you act in life.

_____

_____

_____

_____

_____

_____

_____

_____

_____

_____

_____

Journaling Time

BEING *ZONE* COMMITMENT JOURNALING EXERCISE #56:

What commitments can you make to increase the amount of time you are spending in *The BEING Zone?*

_____

_____

_____

_____

_____

_____

_____

Be specific about when you will build these new activities into your schedule, so they happen.

_____

_____

_____

_____

_____

_____

_____

CHAPTER 6

Discovering Your True North

"I find the great thing in this world is, not so much
where we stand, as in what direction we are moving."
—Goethe

I N C H A P T E R 6, you identify your natural attributes and passions so you can clarify your True North, aka your life's purpose. Throughout this chapter you become much clearer on who you are by examining your life intimately, revealing what you are meant to do in this world, which helps you trust your instincts and intuition. You also are asked to mine and dig deep into the core of who you are, to discover jewels in your life experiences that you may have been unaware of. These journal exercises will assist you through that process and guide you to your internal knowing, so you can clearly define your life's journey with purpose and fulfillment.

Journaling Time

EXCAVATING YOUR LIFE JOURNALING EXERCISE #57:

1. **Who Do You Admire?** List three to five people you admire the most in the world. They can be friends, family, or famous. They may have passed or are alive and well. You do not have to like every single thing about them, but you must genuinely admire something about what they say or do. Make a list of the three to five people you feel are truly amazing. Write about the qualities that you like in each of them. Why do you like them? What is unique about them? What makes them special to you?

_____

_____

_____

_____

_____

_____

_____

_____

_____

_____

_____

_____

2. **List Your Peculiarities, Idiosyncrasies, and Flaws (PIFS).** This is one of your most essential exercises. Honesty is the key, so detail all that you can think of. When you have run out of ideas, ask your spouse or family to help you add to your list. What do you do that drives your family or friends nuts? It might be something as simple as you always interrupt, or you always second guess yourself. Maybe you have to have a clean kitchen before starting to cook. These PIFS are so innate in you that you don't even realize you do it.

_____

_____

_____

_____

_____

_____

_____

_____

_____

_____

_____

_____

_____

_____

3. **What Drives You Nuts About Other People?** As above, list as much here
    as you can think of. You could start your sentences "I dislike it when…"

_____

_____

_____

_____

_____

_____

_____

_____

_____

_____

_____

_____

_____

_____

_____

_____

_____

_____

_____

4. **What Causes Do You Care Most About?** What are the top one or two causes in the world that hurt you or affect you at a deep level? These are the issues where you might feel real pain in your heart when you hear about them. They are the things you want someone to do something about or wish you could do more to resolve.

_____

_____

_____

_____

_____

_____

_____

5. **What Did You Love to Do as a Child?** Think about your childhood ages two to seven. How did you spend your time where you would be lost in the moment and so happy that the day would fly by? If you don't remember your earliest years, ask a family member who might.

_____

_____

_____

_____

_____

6. **Reconnect with the Joys of Your Early Years.** Looking back on your entire life, what were your favorite times, activities, and memories? What filled you up the most or made you the happiest?

_____

_____

_____

_____

_____

_____

_____

7. **What is Your Legacy?** What would you want people to say about you? What do you want to be remembered for?

_____

_____

_____

_____

_____

_____

_____

8. **"Ask Open-Ended Questions."** What energizes you today? What drains
    you? What industries or jobs excite you when you think about them?
    What type of work or jobs would you hate doing? What buzzwords
    energize you? What words depress you? What do you feel your great-
    est strengths are? What are your weaknesses? What are your top three
    work-related favorite memories, where you felt excited or energized?

_____

_____

_____

_____

_____

_____

_____

_____

_____

_____

_____

_____

_____

_____

_____

_____

_____

Journaling Time

THE HEART CHAMBER JOURNALING EXERCISE #58:

Once you listen to the Heart Chamber recording in Chapter 6 at www.The-BEINGZone.com/tools and are ready, write about what you heard, experienced, felt, and learned during the Heart Chamber visualization. This exercise may provide some real ah-ha's for you.

_____

_____

_____

_____

_____

_____

_____

_____

_____

_____

_____

_____

_____

_____

Journaling Time

MOVIE DIRECTOR EXPERIENCE JOURNALING EXERCISE #59:

Write about what you heard, experienced, felt, and learned during the Movie Director visualization found at www.TheBEINGZone.com/tools in Chapter 6. This exercise will help you identify issues to release and ideas on where you might be headed.

_____

_____

_____

_____

_____

_____

_____

_____

_____

_____

_____

_____

_____

MIRROR JOURNALING EXERCISE #60:

What did you feel, experience, and learn during the Mirror Exercise visualization found in Chapter 6 at www.TheBEINGZone.com/tools. Make notes on what you can change in your life to incorporate your key ah-ha's from this session. This Mirror Exercise will help you identify issues to release as well as provide visuals of what you do want.

_____

_____

_____

_____

_____

_____

_____

_____

_____

_____

_____

_____

Journaling Time

**YOUR ANSWERS AND FEELINGS FOR PROCESSING
JOURNALING EXERCISE #61:**

It's time to process your homework.

Who Do You Admire: Take time to highlight all the words you wrote about who you admire and summarize that is into a paragraph that speaks to your heart. This paragraph is a description of you and who you truly are. The sum of the 5 people you admire most is who you are at the core.

_____

_____

_____

_____

_____

_____

_____

_____

_____

_____

_____

_____

_____

Processing Your Peculiarities, Idiosyncrasies, and Flaws: Look at the list you made and group like statements or things together. You can arrange them in bubbles or a spreadsheet. When that is done, you want to create a title for each group that identifies the benefits of those particular PIF's. You can choose to capture your groupings in bubbles. Then let's go ahead and make 5 bubbles on this page and make them as large as you can.

You can choose to capture your PIF's in a spreadsheet, use blank chart below.

You have just processed your Excavating Your Life Homework and you have a better idea of who you are and what's important. Now we are going to review life issues you journaled about and how they affected you. When you read back through all your journaling, notice when your words or descriptions cause an emotional reaction in your body or heart. There will be some things that when you re-read them, make your heart sing, or you may feel a deep sadness, or you may feel irritated or angry. Highlight these and note your reaction. Color code your reactions by what fills you up or makes you happy (yellow highlight) and what drags you down (blue highlight). These are important to know as you move forward in life. Make summary notes on these here.

_____

_____

_____

_____

_____

_____

_____

_____

_____

_____

_____

_____

_____

_____

Use the tools learned in Chapter 3 to continue clearing or *SHIFTING* what drags you down. Group the things that drag you down together from your highlighted list and decide what tools might work best to clear these issues. Make notes on what tools you used and how effective it was for you. Write down all the items that fill you up will need to be considered as we continue to identify your True North.

_____

_____

_____

_____

_____

_____

_____

_____

_____

_____

_____

_____

_____

_____

_____

_____

_____

_____

_____

What Drives You Nuts:

Take all the items you listed in What Drives you Nuts. group them into like categories so you add them to the above PIF bubble or spreadsheet. You will find they usually fall in line with the titles you created for PIF's.

_____

_____

_____

_____

_____

_____

_____

Your Causes and Passions:

Look at the list of issues in the world you identified as really affecting you along with your passions and what energizes you. Look at the titles in the bubbles or chart you made and see if it fits. Most likely they do. Add these to your bubbles or spreadsheet.

_____

_____

_____

_____

_____

_____

Journaling Time

PROCESSING THE GOING DEEP JOURNALING EXERCISES #62:

Review your Journaling exercises #58- 60, the Heart Chamber, Movie Director and Mirror. These deep explorations hopefully shed more light on what you need to clear or how you need to proceed. Reflect on what overall meaning and messages you received from these exercises. Also think about if you had any dreams or inspirations come to you during meditations. If you did, write about how they apply to the bigger picture in your life.

_____

_____

_____

_____

_____

_____

_____

_____

_____

_____

_____

_____

_____

_____

Make notes on the most important ah-ha's.

_____

_____

_____

_____

_____

_____

_____

_____

_____

_____

Make a few notes on things you want to address in your life.

_____

_____

_____

_____

_____

_____

_____

_____

_____

_____

PART III

Connecting
With Source

CHAPTER 7

We Are Energetic Beings

"The energy of the mind is the essence of life".
—Aristotle

I N CHAPTER 7, you'll discover you are connected to everyone and everything and nothing is impossible, which will help you point your life in the direction of your dreams. It has been known for many millennia that people are energetic beings, and this chapter will give you hands-on experience feeling energy and going over the details of how you can level up your life by being aware of your energy. These journal exercises are intended to give you real experience that you can replicate over and over and even grow stronger in your ability to feel energy as you practice.

Journaling Time

RUBBING HANDS TOGETHER JOURNALING EXERCISE #63:

What did you feel on this exercise? Describe the sensations.

_____

_____

_____

_____

_____

Write about all the times you might rub your hands together. For instance if you are nervous before a big speech, or when you are nervous or worried about something. What you are doing is causing friction which helps release the pent up stress energy but also is calming you by increasing the warmth or good energy in your body.

_____

_____

_____

_____

_____

_____

_____

Journaling Time

Tai Chi Ball Journaling Exercise #64:

What did you feel between your hands? Describe the sensations. Was is stronger or weaker than what it felt like when you rubbed your hands together?

_____

_____

_____

_____

_____

Write about how you can consciously build either these exercises into your daily life to calm or increase your energy.

_____

_____

_____

_____

_____

_____

_____

Journaling Time

STAND ON EARTH JOURNALING EXERCISE #65:

You want to stand barefoot on the earths surface (not pavement). Stand in grass, dirt, or sand and pay attention to what you feel. Could you feel anything? Describe your experience.

_____

_____

_____

_____

_____

_____

_____

_____

If you felt something, describe the sensations you felt through the bottom of your feet.

_____

_____

_____

_____

_____

Journaling Time

LEAN AGAINST A TREE JOURNALING EXERCISE #66:

You can stand and lean against a tree or sit up against it. Close your eyes, take a few deep breaths and pay attention to how it feels. Could you feel anything? If so, what did you feel? How would you describe it? Write about how you can build this simple exercise into your current routine.

_____

_____

_____

_____

_____

_____

_____

_____

_____

_____

_____

_____

_____

Journaling Time

DESCRIBE TIMES YOU FELT NEGATIVE
ENERGY JOURNALING EXERCISE #67:

List all the situations you can think of where you felt bad energy.

_____

_____

_____

_____

_____

_____

_____

What did bad energy feel like to you? How would you describe it?

_____

_____

_____

_____

_____

_____

_____

_____

Explain some of the situations you were in where you felt bad energy and write about how you can avoid these types of situations in the future.

_____

_____

_____

_____

_____

_____

_____

_____

How did each of those situations make you feel? Physically? Mentally? Emotionally?

_____

_____

_____

_____

_____

_____

_____

_____

Journaling Time

FILL YOUR VASE JOURNALING EXERCISE #68:

Identify anything or anyone that you want to begin to close out of your life or build boundaries with so you can begin to stop your energy from draining. Make conscious decisions to start the process.

_____

_____

_____

_____

_____

_____

Identify everything that fills you up and make plans to bring more of that into your life.

_____

_____

_____

_____

_____

_____

_____

Make notes on the difference you feel in your life as a result of beginning to make these decisions and changes.

_____

_____

_____

_____

_____

_____

_____

_____

_____

_____

_____

_____

_____

_____

_____

_____

_____

_____

_____

_____

_____

_____

_____

Journaling Time

WHAT CAN YOU CHANGE JOURNALING EXERCISE #69:

Write about people or situations that make you feel bad. Make commitments to change what you can.

_____

_____

_____

_____

_____

_____

Write about people who fill you up and you like to be around. Make decisions to spend more time with them.

_____

_____

_____

_____

_____

_____

_____

_____

Make notes on places in your life where you feel stuck or unhappy. What can you clean up or change?

_____

_____

_____

_____

_____

_____

List areas in your life where you can start standing up for yourself.

_____

_____

_____

_____

_____

_____

Take a look at each item on the list and think about how you can turn it around. Make notes on what you feel you can commit to.

_____

_____

_____

_____

_____

_____

Journaling Time

SMUDGING JOURNALING EXERCISE #70:

Have you done smudging before? Or did you try smudging for the first time after reading this section?

_____

_____

_____

Did you like the smell? Did you like the experience? Did you feel any different?

_____

_____

_____

_____

Describe any observations or feelings you had during or after smudging.

_____

_____

_____

_____

MAGNET IN THE BUBBLE JOURNALING EXERCISE #71:

Go to www.TheBEINGZone.com/tools in Chapter 7 to listen. How did this Magnet in the Bubble tool work for you? Most people feel instant relief. If that was not the case, try again.

_____

_____

_____

_____

_____

If you did feel lighter, describe how you felt.

_____

_____

_____

_____

Write about your plan to utilize this tool in your life.

_____

_____

_____

Journaling Time

WATERFALL JOURNALING EXERCISE #72:

Go to page 228 of *The BEING Zone* book to familiarize yourself with this tool. Did you like this Waterfall tool? Did you feel lighter?

_____

_____

_____

_____

_____

If you did feel lighter, describe how you felt.

_____

_____

_____

_____

_____

Write about your plan to utilize this tool in your life.

_____

_____

_____

Journaling Time

Golden Vacuum Journaling Exercise #73:

Go to www.TheBEINGZone.com/tools for the Golden Vacuum recording. Did you feel lighter from this exercise? If that was not the case, try again.

_____

_____

_____

_____

_____

If you did feel lighter, describe how you felt.

_____

_____

_____

_____

Write about your plan to utilize this tool in your life.

_____

_____

_____

CUTTING ENERGETIC CORDS JOURNALING EXERCISE #74:

Go to www.TheBEINGZone.com/tools for the recording. Could you visualize and see the cords dropping? If not, try again. If you did, describe how you felt.

_____

_____

_____

_____

_____

_____

_____

_____

_____

_____

Write about your plan to utilize this tool in your life.

_____

_____

_____

_____

Journaling Time

WHITE LIGHT OF PROTECTION JOURNALING EXERCISE #75:

Go to www.TheBEINGZone.com/tools for the recording. Could you visualize this light? Did you feel a difference?

_____

_____

_____

_____

_____

Describe how you felt.

_____

_____

_____

_____

_____

Write about your plan to utilize this tool in your life.

_____

_____

_____

Journaling Time

MIRROR SHIELDING JOURNALING EXERCISE #76:

Go to www.TheBEINGZone.com/tools for the recording. Could you visualize the mirrors? Did it work for you?

_____

_____

_____

_____

_____

Describe how you felt.

_____

_____

_____

_____

Write about your plan to utilize this tool in your life.

_____

_____

_____

Journaling Time

FORTRESS OR WALL PROTECTION JOURNALING EXERCISE #77:

Go to www.TheBEINGZone.com/tools for the recording. Could you visualize the barrier? Did you feel protected?

_____

_____

_____

_____

_____

Describe how you felt.

_____

_____

_____

_____

Write about your plan to utilize this tool in your life.

_____

_____

_____

Journaling Time

ROOT, RELEASE, & RECEIVE JOURNALING EXERCISE #78:

Go to www.TheBEINGZone.com/tools for the Root, Release & Receive recording. Write about how it feels to be rooted or connected to the earth.

_____

_____

_____

_____

_____

_____

_____

Note how it feels to be able to release or drain all the negative, heavy energy.

_____

_____

_____

_____

_____

_____

_____

Write about how it feels to fill up with golden, vibrating Universal energy.

_____

_____

_____

_____

_____

_____

_____

_____

_____

Write about how you will build this process into your life.

_____

_____

_____

_____

_____

_____

_____

_____

_____

_____

Journaling Time

EARTHING/GROUNDING JOURNALING EXERCISE #79:

Have you ever felt the life force of the ground vibrating through your body, making you feel part of the greater whole?

_____

_____

_____

_____

_____

Where in nature do you feel alive? Which of the following are you more drawn to: oceans, rivers, desert, forest, mountains, or where else? Each of these natural terrains brings something to the individual seeking connection, seeking calm, seeking health.

_____

_____

_____

_____

_____

_____

_____

Think about all of the natural places you love to be at and write about which one is your favorite and why.

_____

_____

_____

_____

_____

Go outside and sit in the grass or on the beach and take time to tune in with your senses. What does it feel like? What does it look like? What does it smell like? What do you hear? What do you see? How do you feel?

_____

_____

_____

_____

_____

Write about how you will build Grounding into your daily life.

_____

_____

_____

_____

_____

_____

Journaling Time

CONNECT WITH UNIVERSAL ENERGY JOURNALING EXERCISE #80:

Take the time to go outside and connect with the moon, stars, and constellations. Journal on how it feels and what you experienced. Keep practicing until you know without a doubt that you are experiencing the energy from this activity.

_____

_____

_____

_____

_____

_____

_____

_____

_____

Write about you will utilize how you will utilize this tool moving forward.

_____

_____

_____

_____

Journaling Time

CREATE A LIST OF THINGS AND PEOPLE YOU LOVE JOURNALING EXERCISE #81:

Make a list of things and activities that you love to do.

_____

_____

_____

_____

_____

_____

Make a list of all the people from home, family, friends, work, and the community who make you happy. Who do you enjoy being around and feel better after spending time with them?

_____

_____

_____

_____

_____

Create an intention and plan to spend more time with them and put specific commitments into your calendar.

_____

_____

_____

_____

_____

_____

_____

_____

_____

_____

_____

_____

_____

_____

_____

_____

_____

_____

_____

_____

_____

_____

Journaling Time

TREE GROUNDING VISUALIZATION JOURNALING EXERCISE #82:

Go to www.TheBEINGZone.com/tools for the Tree Grounding recording. How did the Tree Grounding Visualization feel to you?

_____

_____

_____

_____

_____

_____

Could you feel the energy flow through your entire body? If not, how far could you feel it? Could you feel it in your legs? Your core? Your neck and head? Each time you do this practice, you will get stronger and able to take it further up through your body's energy system.

_____

_____

_____

_____

_____

Write about your experience and plan to continue to use this tool.

_____

_____

_____

_____

_____

_____

_____

_____

_____

_____

_____

_____

_____

_____

_____

_____

_____

_____

_____

_____

_____

_____

_____

_____

Journaling Time

**BREATHE AND TIGHTEN ENERGY CENTERS
JOURNALING EXERCISE #83:**

Go to www.TheBEINGZone.com/tools for the Breathe and Tighten recording. When you tightened each energy center, did you feel anything in that specific area? Describe what you experienced.

_____

_____

_____

Could you feel the difference of energy or flow through your body as you tightened each area? Talk about how it made you feel.

_____

_____

_____

When might you use this tool moving forward?

_____

_____

_____

_____

Journaling Time

BREATH OF FIRE JOURNALING EXERCISE #84:

Go to www.TheBEINGZone.com/tools for the Breath of Fire recording. What was different for you with the Breath of Fire compared to what you experienced with other breathing exercises?

_____

_____

_____

_____

_____

How did it make your body feel?

_____

_____

_____

_____

_____

_____

_____

_____

Journaling Time

ENERGY MOVEMENTS JOURNALING EXERCISE #85:

What are the energy movements that you can commit to or try? Yoga? Tai Chi? Qigong? Other?

_____

_____

_____

_____

Find the one that works best for you and build it into your schedule. Make notes here on how you plan to incorporate at least one of these modalities into your life.

_____

_____

_____

_____

_____

_____

_____

Journaling Time

TUNE INTO ENERGY JOURNALING EXERCISE #86:

When you have good energy flow in your body and are asking questions, your body will respond. It will feel more flow if the idea resonates with you and you will feel a tightness or a decrease in flow if the idea is not good. Take some time fill your body with energy and ask questions and journal about what you hear or feel.

_____

_____

_____

_____

_____

_____

_____

_____

_____

_____

_____

_____

_____

_____

_____

Connecting
With Source

"All Creation Is One so people should try to
live a simple life in harmony with nature and
with others. I am part or particle of God."
—Ralph Waldo Emerson

I n Chapter 8, you learn about how you are an energetic being connected to the universe and now you'll visit
the concept of connecting with that Universal Source energy and
how it can impact your life. When you learn the exercises presented
and integrate them into your life your circumstances can dramatically change for you. These journal exercises will help you document your connection with a Source greater than yourself and give
you the opportunity to start receiving guidance on a regular basis.

Journaling Time

YOU CAN CONNECT JOURNALING EXERCISE #87:

Write about when you feel more connected to yourself or a greater Source.

_____

_____

_____

_____

_____

_____

_____

Pay attention to your surroundings, the situation, the time of day, the sounds, and how you feel when you are feeling a connection with Source. The more you are aware of what works for you, the more you can build on this skill.

_____

_____

_____

_____

_____

_____

_____

Write about your experiences when connecting with Source.

_____

_____

_____

_____

_____

_____

_____

_____

_____

_____

_____

_____

_____

_____

_____

_____

_____

_____

_____

_____

_____

_____

_____

Journaling Time

VISUALIZATION PRACTICE JOURNALING EXERCISE #88:

Follow the steps for visualization practices on pages 259 and 260 in *The BEING Zone* book and document what you felt, thought, and experienced.

_____

_____

_____

_____

_____

Were you able to visualize and experience what you expected based on the descriptions? Write about it.

_____

_____

_____

_____

_____

_____

_____

_____

Journaling Time

WHAT ENERGY FEELS LIKE TO YOU JOURNALING EXERCISE #89:

Describe what it feels like to you when you are in good energy or bring energy into your body. This is a feeling you want to learn to expand.

_____

_____

_____

_____

_____

_____

_____

_____

_____

_____

_____

_____

_____

_____

_____

_____

_____

_____

Journaling Time

LIGHT VERSUS DARK JOURNALING EXERCISE #90:

Revisit pages 262 and 263 in *The BEING Zone* book to refresh yourself on light vs. dark. Do you tend to operate more in what I call the light (good or positive energy)? Describe what you feel.

_____

_____

_____

_____

Or are you more in the dark (bad or negative energy)? Describe what you feel.

_____

_____

_____

_____

Just observe yourself and write about your tendencies to increase your awareness.

_____

_____

_____

_____

Journaling Time

DO YOU LOVE YOURSELF JOURNALING EXERCISE #91:

Do you love yourself? What does that look like?

_____

_____

_____

_____

_____

_____

_____

How does self-love feel to you?

_____

_____

_____

_____

_____

_____

_____

Journaling Time

FORGIVE AND LOVE JOURNALING EXERCISE #92:

Who do you need to forgive in your life? Make some notes and think about all the people in your life who you feel wronged by, then work through the forgiveness process on each person that hurt you.

_____

_____

_____

_____

_____

_____

_____

_____

_____

_____

_____

_____

_____

_____

_____

_____

_____

What do you need to forgive yourself for?

_____

_____

_____

_____

_____

_____

_____

_____

_____

Write about how it felt to forgive yourself and all others.

_____

_____

_____

_____

_____

_____

_____

_____

_____

_____

_____

Journaling Time

LOCATION JOURNALING EXERCISE #93:

Write down several locations where you can be comfortable connecting with
Source energy. Look around your home and community and decide on the
places where you feel most grounded and feel you would have the ability to
connect, whether it be with the Universe or the Earth.

_____

_____

_____

_____

_____

List several options depending on weather or time of year to ensure you stay
comfortable.

_____

_____

_____

_____

_____

_____

Write about what time of day is best for you. I like early morning but figure out what time of day works for you.

_____

_____

_____

_____

_____

Make a commitment to days and times you will connect and write it down.

_____

_____

_____

_____

_____

_____

_____

_____

_____

_____

_____

_____

_____

_____

Journaling Time

CONNECTING WITH SOURCE ENERGY AND REPLACING FEELINGS JOURNALING EXERCISE #94:

Make notes on how well the Connecting with Source Energy and Replace Feelings exercise worked for you. Did you have any ah-ha's or messages that came to you?

_____

_____

_____

_____

_____

_____

Did you feel a connection? What did that feel like for you?

_____

_____

_____

_____

_____

_____

_____

Did you feel like you were able to change how you felt physically, mentally, or emotionally? Write about that. Is this an exercise you will use moving forward?

_____

_____

_____

_____

_____

_____

What was the time of day or location where you felt most connected?

_____

_____

_____

_____

_____

_____

What steps worked best for you? How did you get to that place of connection?

_____

_____

_____

_____

_____

_____

What did you feel? What did you hear or learn?

_____

_____

_____

_____

_____

_____

_____

_____

_____

_____

_____

_____

_____

_____

_____

_____

_____

_____

_____

_____

_____

_____

_____

PART IV

Creating a Life
You Love!

CHAPTER 9

Happiness-Boosting Activities

"One of the first conditions of happiness is that the
link between man and nature shall not be broken."
—Leo Tolstoy

CHAPTER 9 GIVES you the opportunity to identify happiness-boosting hobbies and activities you will genuinely enjoy, and the tools needed to integrate them into your life. This is really important for you to feel energized, satisfied, and excited for each day. Incorporating happiness-boosting activities will dramatically change your level of happiness because you will be feeding your heart's desires and not just getting by or doing what has to be done. This is truly self-care, and when you are full of joy and happiness you are better suited to share that with your family, friends, and in your career. These journaling exercises will give you a chance to try out different activities to find which ones you like best, as they will be different for everyone.

Journaling Time

WHAT DRAINS YOU JOURNALING EXERCISE #95:

Write about what drains you in your life. Is it your job, your friends, your family, how you spend your time?

_____

_____

_____

_____

_____

_____

_____

Identify what is no longer working for you once you understand all the things that can drain you.

_____

_____

_____

_____

_____

_____

_____

What fills you up?

_____

_____

_____

_____

_____

Make a commitment to exchange a draining activity with something that fills you up. Write about what that would be.

_____

_____

_____

_____

_____

_____

_____

_____

_____

_____

_____

_____

_____

Journaling Time

CAREER ENRICHMENT JOURNALING EXERCISE #96:

Think about and document what you love to do at work or what you love about your job.

_____

_____

_____

_____

_____

Take time to identify things you can do during your work breaks that will re-fuel or energize you. It could be things as simple as taking a stretching break or walking at lunch with friends or building in work activities that you enjoy.

_____

_____

_____

_____

_____

_____

_____

_____

What do you love about your company culture, co-workers or teammates? If you take time to think about what you like about the culture, when times are troubled, you can stay focused on what you do like. Make a list of all the things you like about your company and its environment. Keep this list in mind when you get frustrated at work. Examples might be you like the location of your job because it is near trails or shops or has beautiful grounds. Or you might like the décor inside because its calming.

_____

_____

_____

_____

_____

_____

_____

_____

_____

_____

_____

_____

_____

_____

_____

_____

_____

_____

Write down how many hours you can commit to your career on a daily basis and still maintain happiness. You want to keep it at a reasonable level so you can spend more time doing activities that fill you up outside of work.

_____

_____

_____

_____

_____

_____

_____

Journal about how much time you spend working and brainstorm ways you may be able to be more efficient so you can spend more time doing activities that fill you up outside of work. Make a list of what some of those activities might be.

_____

_____

_____

_____

_____

_____

_____

_____

Review your notes in your notebook or *BEING Journal* from Chapter 6 around your purpose and fulfillment to help you move forward in your career. Once you refresh your memory, begin journaling about what conscious decisions you can make to improve your work life, job, or career to make it more fulfilling whether it be learning new things or cross-training in another area.

_____

_____

_____

_____

_____

_____

Now that you have more clarity around your purpose or what is fulfilling to you, is that part of your current job? If not, can you build it into your current work or life by volunteering or having a new hobby? Write about changes you will make.

_____

_____

_____

_____

_____

_____

_____

_____

Or is it time to start looking for a new career? Consider working with us or a Career Coach to begin to plan your next step based on your answers. Make notes on how you will approach this and what is important to you in your next job or career.

_____

_____

_____

_____

_____

_____

_____

_____

_____

_____

_____

_____

_____

_____

_____

_____

_____

_____

_____

Journaling Time

Happiness-Boosting Activities for Health and Wellness Journaling Exercise #97:

Write about spending time in nature or outside and how it feels to you. Write about your Grounding experience if you got outside to try it.

_____

_____

_____

_____

_____

_____

Write about your Qigong or Yoga experience if you got online and tried it out or took a class. Talk about how you might build Qigong or yoga into your life.

_____

_____

_____

_____

_____

_____

Describe how you can build more meditation into your life. Think about the time of day, the source of the meditation. What is your favorite part of meditation?

_____

_____

_____

_____

_____

_____

_____

_____

Identify some relaxation exercises that resonate with you and describe how it makes you feel and how you might be able to build a meditation practice into your life.

_____

_____

_____

_____

_____

_____

_____

_____

What experiences have you had with sound healing? How did it feel during and after? Is this something that is a good match for you? If so, make notes on how you will build sound healing into your life.

_____

_____

_____

_____

_____

_____

_____

Think about what diet changes may be the most beneficial for you and write about it. What healthy foods can you add to your diet? What do you want to delete from your diet?

_____

_____

_____

_____

_____

_____

_____

_____

_____

What supplements may be the most beneficial for you? Is it time to see your doctor or naturopath to help you make these decisions?

_____

_____

_____

_____

_____

_____

_____

Make notes on what physical, mental, or emotional issues are impacting your life most. Then do an online search to see which essential oils would be helpful in your healing process. You want to be sure you are using therapeutic grade oils to ensure the best results.

_____

_____

_____

_____

_____

_____

_____

Describe the aches, pain, ailments, and illnesses you would like to correct in your body. Then search online as to which acupressure points would be most useful for you, or you can schedule an appointment with a reflexologist or acupressure specialist or acupuncturist for treatment. Create a daily regimen of the points you would like to focus on if you are going to do acupressure on yourself.

_____

_____

_____

_____

_____

_____

_____

_____

Write about your sleep habits and do some research on what might help you the most. Bear in mind that essential oils and acupressure can be very effective.

_____

_____

_____

_____

_____

_____

_____

_____

What are the health and wellness activities you already do that are not on the list?

_____

_____

_____

_____

_____

_____

_____

_____

_____

_____

_____

_____

_____

_____

_____

_____

_____

_____

_____

_____

_____

_____

_____

_____

Journaling Time

HAPPINESS-BOOSTING ACTIVITIES FOR
SPIRITUALITY JOURNALING EXERCISE #98:

Write down how you will build Grounding into your life to increase your connection with Source.

_____

_____

_____

_____

Write about how you plan to build connecting with Source into your life.

_____

_____

_____

_____

Write about your current prayer practices or the new ones you would like to adopt.

_____

_____

_____

_____

Journaling Time

RELATIONSHIP BUILDING JOURNALING EXERCISE #99:

Write about which type of relationship building activities you might enjoy the most. They may not be included in the above list as everyone has different interests. Make a commitment to at least one activity that you can begin building into your life today!

Write about what activities you love to do, inside and out, with other people so you can strengthen relationships.

What are some of your favorite games and who might be interested in playing games with you?

_____

_____

_____

Identify potential friends to have book club or movie night with to bring more enrichment into your life.

_____

_____

_____

What groups or clubs can you join?

_____

_____

_____

Are there any classes or events you have an interest in that you could plan on attending?

_____

_____

_____

_____

_____

Journaling Time

HAPPINESS-BOOSTING ACTIVITIES TO
INCORPORATE JOURNALING EXERCISE #100:

Which Happiness-Boosting activities would work the best for you? Make a commitment to add one or two of these to your daily routine.

_____

_____

_____

_____

Are you open to arts, crafts or music? If so, which?

_____

_____

_____

_____

Do you like to write? What type of writing activities can you build into your life?

_____

_____

_____

_____

Who do you love to spend time with? How can it help you?

_____

_____

_____

_____

Do you have a gratitude journal? Do you use it? Can you commit to trying this? Write about what you will commit to now.

_____

_____

_____

_____

What activities can you add to your life that will keep you active or outdoors in nature?

_____

_____

_____

_____

What new things can you try?

_____

_____

_____

_____

CHAPTER 10

The 5 Daily B.E.I.N.G. Steps

"We carry inside us the wonders we seek outside us."
—Rumi

HAPTER 10 GOES over, in detail, the 5 Daily B.E.I.N.G Steps. When this practice becomes a part of your routine, you will feel better, happier, and more able to enjoy life in general. Starting your day with this routine will also give you a solid foundation to work from and start you off on the right foot and maintain your ability to stay in *The BEING Zone*. Our clients tell us it is this step that makes a real difference as to whether they have a good day or a bad day. You want to make your daily practice a habit. Over time you will become more and more connected, intuitive, and aware of your innate needs and even start to live from your heart's desires with more ease. Your true divine nature will reveal itself over time and what a joy that will be. These journal exercises will help you set up your 5 Daily B.E.I.N.G Steps.

Journaling Time

SAMPLE DAILY PRACTICE JOURNALING EXERCISE #101:

First practice utilizing the sample daily practice steps on pages 307 to 313 of *The BEING Zone* book and make notes on what worked for you.

_____

_____

_____

_____

_____

_____

Document what parts you liked best and what you might change when you customize it.

_____

_____

_____

_____

_____

_____

_____

_____

Journaling Time

YOUR PLAN FOR YOUR "B" STEP FOR THE B.E.I.NG.
PRACTICE JOURNALING EXERCISE #102:

Review the section about customizing your B for BEING Step practice on pages 314 through 322 in *The BEING Zone* book and choose what activities resonate most with you. Write those down and include in your customized plan below to ensure it is part of your daily practice. Put reminders for your daily practice into your calendar and add your notes to your notepad for ease of access.

_____

_____

_____

_____

_____

_____

_____

_____

_____

_____

_____

_____

Journaling Time

YOUR PLAN FOR STEP "E" OF THE DAILY B.E.I.NG.
PRACTICE JOURNALING EXERCISE #103:

Review the options for the E or Energy Step of your practice on pages 322 -
325 of *The BEING Zone* Book. Then add any other energy tools you learned in
Chapter 7, and journal about which ones you will begin to use on a daily basis.
If you plan to use your cell phone Notepad like I do, add these notes there also.

Journaling Time

YOUR "I" STEP IN YOUR DAILY B.E.I.NG.
PRACTICE JOURNALING EXERCISE #104:

Refer to pages 325-328 of *The BEING Zone* book for ideas for Intentions. Your intentions are the most likely things to continue to change in your daily practice. Write the ones that are most appropriate for you today and just know as you achieve things, you will be updating these to keep you moving forward.

_____

_____

_____

_____

_____

_____

Write about how you will build your gratefulness into this, on the front end to help make the intention happen and on the hind end after you have achieved it.

_____

_____

_____

_____

_____

Journaling Time

YOUR "N" STEP IN YOUR DAILY B.E.I.NG.
PRACTICE JOURNALING EXERCISE #105:

Decide on your purpose by reviewing pages 329-331 and Chapter 6 in *The BEING Zone* book and and build your affirmation statements and visualizations of it happening into your daily work and add to your notepad.

_____

_____

_____

_____

_____

_____

_____

_____

_____

_____

_____

_____

_____

_____

_____

Journaling Time

YOUR "G" STEP OF YOUR DAILY B.E.I.NG.
PRACTICE JOURNALING EXERCISE #106:

Capture the exact words and sentences you will say and feel into as part of your
daily practice for connecting with Source. When you sit with those words and
are quiet, you will begin to get guidance. Revisit page 331-333 in *The BEING
Zone* book to help you with this.

_____

_____

_____

_____

_____

_____

_____

_____

_____

_____

_____

_____

_____

_____

Open Journaling

A PLACE WHERE YOU CAN WRITE ANYTHING THAT WASN'T CAPTURED
IN ALL THE JOURNALING ASSIGNMENTS YOU HAVE BEEN THROUGH.

_____

_____

_____

_____

_____

_____

_____

_____

_____

_____

_____

_____

_____

_____

_____

_____

_____

_____

_____

_____

_____

About the Authors

Marla Williams is a coach, speaker, and spiritual intuitive who guides people to happiness and health through a self-discovery, reconnection, and the healing process. Marla is passionate about helping people transform their lives by learning to operate in *The BEING Zone*. She wrote The *BEING Zone* book, has a coaching practice and an online training program to accomplish this. Learn more at www.TheBEINGZone.com. She lives on an island in the Pacific Northwest with her husband Mark and dog Mack.

Amanda Stovall is an intuitive life coach, teacher, and artist with a heart of compassion. She helps unlock people's hearts in whatever way they need to be able to move forward in their lives. The core of her teaching and expression is based on the foundation of self-love and acceptance. Amanda co-authored this journal and *The BEING Zone* Online Training Program with Marla because she wants to empower others to live their best and most meaningful lives.

Training and Certification:

I F YOU ARE a Coach, Psychologist, Therapist, or work in a related field where you work with clients to help them transform their lives, you will benefit from being trained and certified in *The BEING Zone System*. Individuals will also benefit from taking this training to work on improving their own lives by learning to exist in *The BEING Zone*. If you are interested and ready to become certified as a *BEING Zone* Practitioner, go to www.TheBEINGZone.com to find a class schedule or online class that meets your needs.

Made in the USA
Monee, IL
12 October 2020